Arboretum in a Jar

Frances Donovan

LILY POETRY REVIEW BOOKS

Library of Congress Control Number: 2022948851

Cover design and Layout: Michael d'Entremont McInnis

ISBN: 978-1-957755-17-5

Published by Lily Poetry Review Books
223 Winter Street
Whitman, MA 02382
https://lilypoetryreview.blog/

For Mark, my happy ending

Acknowledgments

Many thanks to the editors of the following journals who published these poems, sometimes in different iterations. You are the unsung, mostly unpaid heroes of the poetry world. I appreciate your labor of love.

Blanket Sea – "The Window" and "What the Crows Did"

Incessant Pipe – "The Fish Head"

SWWIM Every Day – "A Copy of Szymborska's Collected Poems Abandoned on a Table"

Marathon Literary Review – "The Secrets of Sourdough"

Heavy Feather Review – "Fox News Princess, "What Snow White Swallows," and "Lovers Rapunzel Finds in the Wilderness"

Fire Poetry Journal – "The Marigolds, the River, the Oaks"

Lily Poetry Review – "What a Mess I've Made"

Hare's Paw Literary Journal – "cross-country suite"

Nixes Mate Review – "On the Ferry to Spectacle Island"

Contents

Arboretum in a Jar

ONE

Rapunzel Free of the Tower

And the whole wilderness waiting.
She never searches for the prince.
Her hair grows back.
She buzzes it again and again,
the salty prickle of a freshly shorn scalp.
Here's what she finds: Three bats
floating in the gloaming. Insect bites.
Grocery cart dripping with weeds.
Three bright red berries against
black branches and a crust of snow.
A burning marsh. An island full of bird shit.
An island full of *flamboyan*.
A grassy bank by Route Nine
where she teaches herself the Tarot.
Sunlight rolling down a green slope to the Hudson.
Two toads croaking in the palm of her hand.
Lentils and rice with carrot sticks.
A church full of pagans
and atheists. Harvard Yard's frozen mud
in January, its indifferent trees.
Three cones from the hemlock tree,
dirty and precious in her pocket.
A feral cat who hides in her closet.
A three-decker in February, cold
radiating from the wall into her bedclothes.
Glow of the computer screen
late in the night, what is she seeking,
always seeking.

little princess meets bear meets rabbit meets chicken

party at bear mountain   in the woods
someone spikes the oranges   brother eats one
throws up loud   father laughs and laughs

rabbits in the hutch   how she wants that soft
the chickens cluck and cluck   conceal their eggs

father trims the ivy on the redwood fence   little princess finds an egg
brings it to her mother   she spins it on the countertop
it spins and spins that means   the egg is dead

The Secrets of Sourdough

in the voice of my mother

How the air carries the seed of the bread.
Gold-mad, men in denim pull it from the wind
while they sift the silt from the river.

Down-coast the ships dock,
piled with rice and sailors. Dressed
in white, they descend the gangplanks.

The sun's a bitter pill.
I tear my knees on the asphalt.
When my father comes back to land and dies,

my mother forgets my name.
I meet a man who's mostly naked.
I cook him a pot of won ton soup.

I go to Mexico
but he turns back at the border, his hands
full of peacocks.

When I return he takes me home.
I wake up with him
spreading his wings inside me.

After your brother's born we go north.
My mother-in-law is the one
who gives him the Wild Turkey.

When he spends all our money and the neighbors
shoot the chickens,
I pull bread out of the air to feed you.

What Snow White Swallows

ginger snaps
a matchstick

square pizza in the school cafeteria
her body spreading in the mirror

the white cheek of a poison apple
the red cheek of a poison apple

cookies from the keebler elves
grow up fast

your fault your fault your fault
whole wheat bread

sweet bliss of chocolate
(how it gathers on the tongue and gums

the back of the mouth
turns sour)

gathering scabs
three tabs of acid

doll heads
their china eyes

paring knives
your father ruined our lives

two cups of gin and a cup of juice
what do you mean you don't know how

to lock the door
you should have known

it was an accident
it never happened

day-glo post-it notes
thirty red-and-white pills slick as m&ms

little princess meets disney

start with can't all the things she longs to do but can't
run cry pout rave stomp and stomp and stomp
she can sit like an ornament in a case she can seed and wheedle
she can lay her dresses wide and steep upon the counterpane
she can suffer pine and moan and rain she can't complain

little princess doesn't know pink and fluffy dresses
makes do with scraps of cloth she wraps about
her off-brand barbie dolls *feel this one it feels*
like satin doesn't it is this what satin feels like?

at halloween she trails a whole bedsheet from the top
of her princess mask lips bubblegum pink eyelids sky blue
eyeholes too small to see breath heavy dizzy in the plastic mask

one strange and sticky chicken her companion
or a fox or a cat or a raccoon singing her saccharine
into the mild autumn air the requisite scrubbing and whistling

hips still feet in dainty slippers to sit in the tower to gaze
as through a mirror darkly to prick her finger on the waiting needle
the forgotten godmother the plump rumps of the good fairies
granting her *sit quiet be sweet*

from the tip of her ivory finger squeeze one drop of brilliant red
she'd be safe but for the dragon the poison apple the beast
the clock striking the abandoned slipper the prince
with his braided shoulder standing empty handed

cross-country suite

little princess won't remember very much from california
a row of sunflowers towers above her   she drags a plastic bus
across her gramma's kitchen floor   sienna-pattern tiles

she remembers the dew   on the old white ford at 5am
her brother   wet the bed   she remembers how her father threw
her mother across the front seat   her mother's short, sharp cry

                *   *   *

in connecticut   three towers loom   eighteen stories over asphalt
broken chair and teddy bear   curtains hung with twine
mattress on the floor   and then   a bed   two dressers made of pine

on the balcony they have a picnic   iceberg lettuce   tuna salad
bean sprouts on whole-wheat bread   they sit on wire milk crates
little princess so small   her feet won't touch the floor

draw a picture of how you feel   says mom   her brother draws godzilla
his flaming mouth   a tiny house   what does little princess draw?
a blank spot   what does she draw?   a blank spot

                *   *   *

three cardboard boxes   inside the wedding china   jagged-edged
your gramma packed it wrong so it would break!   yells mom
it sits in its pigeon-nest on the balcony   traffic-dust settles

her dad follows them 3,000 miles   begging
take me back   and so they do

little princess and her brother   build a castle under the bed
dollhouse walls fall apart   shingles and a window
cardboard boxes fill the gaps   ladders up   ladders down

an orphan wall with a door   two stuffed rabbits in pink and blue
off-brand barbie with her rigid arms   gi joe with a window in his head
a plastic cow   they race them up and down the ladders

*   *   *

in the morning her father asks for water   little princess brings him a
    tall glass
he drinks it in one long swallow   his throat working and working
crossing the street   little princess reaches up   to take his hand

and his cigarette burns her   *bright pain!*   the ashy circle pink at the
    center
she keeps mum   doesn't know what drunk is
but knows *stop whining*   is the bottle on the counter

by noon he's slurring   slides open the terrace door   chases the
    pigeons
yells *look at this junk!*   throws the broken china overboard   it sails
six stories to the parking lot   little princess shrieks with glee
or terror   or a blank spot

Aunt Margaret's Hands

Liver-spotted skin, thin
as evenings in Arabia,
turn the pages of *1001 Nights*,
play out a milk jug on a plastic rope
to draw the water pure, and sweet,
from the well, pluck wild onions,
plant lettuce, set the gas ring ticking to heat
sugar and water and strawberries for jam,
chafe the warmth back in our feet
that first winter, cut a paper snowflake,
dance the keys of the wirework typewriter,
pull the rake across the rippled
sand at low tide, expose the clams
and drop them in the wire basket,
slip the knife between the shells' hard lips,
spoon out clam chowder,
cut tomatoes for sandwiches,
flick the coffee grinder chute
at the A&P, hold the dark and earthy scent,
shuffle cards on rainy days, tot up
points for gin rummy,
rest on the windowsill, as rain
makes the double panes wave-heavy.

little princess becomes a pea

without skin she stalks the world   tenderheart   tenderfoot
tender aching back   no one can feel her

it's safe here in the darkness   mattress upon mattress
make her safe   sometimes she's dry   sometimes she has a rock for
    company

sometimes she's a rattle in a can   the witches use her for zar
but nothing comes of it   she just rattles and rattles

Dirt Princess

Longs for fingers in the mycelium,
tiny excavations, piling grime beneath her nails.

Barefoot, the concrete makes her mince, asphalt binds
every garden in this city, she tips across the path with her

pile of weeds, dirt-streaked face, fairy-flecked,
dirt princess must dig down.

TWO

Rapunzel in the Tower

As soon as the witch gets
that shrill in her voice,
Rapunzel leaps to burnish the dishes,
shrive the newspapers, sanctify the counter.
As if some ritual might
ward away the witch's ire.

The witch won't stop yelling
until Rapunzel cries.
Then she's satisfied.
When they're both wrung out, the witch
stares real hard, says,
How can we keep from fighting?

Once Rapunzel's older she'll grapple
with the witch in the doorway,
slam it open and pound down the stairs,
the witch's voice echoing and echoing.

She'll call the prince from a payphone
but now that she's let down her hair
he's off to play D&D with his friends.
Under the arches of the city library,
she'll unearth a story about Petrosinella
trapped in a tower, who stole three gall-nuts
and tricked her way to freedom.

little princess meets the jackal

safe and shiny shopping mall   the counter full of chocolates
Le Croissant with its flaky pastries   stores full of sweaters she can't
    afford

every five minutes the fountain spouts   a tall plume of water
splices the chrome-tipped balconies   she follows it up

there's a skylight   there's a secret hallway with a single store
selling turnips and nasturtiums   the jackal's there with his friends

they corner her   the jackal sniffs and sniffs her
throws her over his shoulder   the cashier rings her up

the jackal drags her home to boil and smash

The Fish Head

Under deep water I found you
in a jar as big as my head.
Boiling and poised to explode,
you made the glass hot in my hands.

She warned me not to,
but I carried you anyway.
Past those sand-colored walls,
the pool you could not swim in,
the shoes you could not wear,
I carried you – my treasure,
my foundling,
my arboretum in a jar.

At the top of the stairs,
your bubbling subsided.
But even in your tower room –
the one that I picked out for you –
you seethe and you simmer,
a veritable forest of tangles.
I wonder if I will ever get you straight.

Snow White Goes to the Void Seven Times

One

What holds the space around the empty space?

Her throat closes on the apple.

The void yawns.

She plummets past cobwebs,
an iridescent shawl hung on a wall. The monster
stalks beyond the membrane. It cannot get through.

Two

In therapy she's crying again.

It will swallow me!

She falls from the embrace of the comfy chair.

Look, says the therapist,
and I'll look with you.

After a while, the void goes away

and she is in the chair again.

Three

There is no falling

because there is no down.

Look into the abyss.

See how stars populate

the empty sky.

See how the space between stars

makes way for god/dess to step through.

Four

So many things not there.

No apples, no oranges, no yell-
owing paper, no small child crying. No crack
of the glass. No you who threw it, no you
who heard it.

No pencils, no knives.

No hammers, no scissors.

No teeth to bite. Bite the void.

The void bites back.

Five

The monster lives in a gray and cloudy light –

full of ashes, yes, but

see how the sink stands where it always has,

the toothbrush in its cup.

Dust and murk, hard
to recognize the edges of the counter,
the doorway, but she can follow the path
to the edge of the swimming pool – empty now, a hole
where the monster lays slug-eggs in the mouth of its prey.

She is the monster. A great toothy flower

instead of a face, five-fold symmetry.

When the mouth of the flower-face

morphs to vagina dentata,

she cuts off its head.

Then the void.

Six

You don't find the void,

the void finds you.

But she tries.

The sharp of Scotch

just takes her sideways.

She tries with the spark-lit pipe.

The smoke envelops her, creeps, penetrates,
smothers her in tingling. She cannot sit straight,
she is falling without falling.

Sex works

for three minutes or so.

Seven

It's a cloud-stop,
a thumping dromping cumulus.
It is thunder over the ocean air.
It is downstairs.

All praises and songs to the void.

Unconscious mind is not it, but it is there.

Up and down the darky stairs

only the void knows how

the void

knows.

The Final Return

Dry, still air in the hot, glass box.
The apple piece unlodged, she chokes.
She wakes.

Rapunzel Locks Her Keys in the Tower

The witch gave Rapunzel keys when she was eleven.
The witch works overtime.

Rapunzel takes the trash to the chute,
hears the door click behind her.

The key is sitting on the kitchen table.
The hallway stinks of cabbage and mold.

The lobby echoes over grimy linoleum,
the front lock's always broken.

She steps outside. The six-lane boulevard,
the strip of tired gingkoes.

Sharp-dark smell of car exhaust.
The back of the Hartman Theater's crumbling bricks.

The sky darkens to cobalt. No coat and no keys.
Traffic thickens and she's adrift.

Feet aching. She paces in the graying light,
down to the plaza across from City Hall. Its staring clock face.

Buses come and go.
Her wallet's in the Tower too.

The library's white columns telescope down Main Street,
past the Chinese restaurant, the bar named Apples

where they'll serve her without carding,
past the Palace Theater where she ushers Saturday nights,

the Landmark Center with the ice rink below street level.
The mall bulks in the distance.

Pacing, prickle on the back of her neck.
Never too long in one place. Knows not to catch

the eyes of the men who pass her by.

What a Mess I've Made

in the voice of my mother

Fever makes it clear –
the socks in the dishwasher, the bills
due last Tuesday propped against the china
in the hutch. I see the mess

but not how to make it neat, which my daughter
always seemed to know, she could set
a great pile of clutter to rights

in an afternoon. Holidays she would chase
me from the kitchen, a paring knife in her hand,
half an onion chopped on the board,
and I knew, I knew the terrible burden

I'd placed on her. How she'd closed up
like an iris in late frost.

Manic Episode Princess

mad dash to the sprinkle-goo
of the daily toothbrush
she throws out the toothbrush

starts writing a novel
about a princess who meets a queen
who meets a knave and also navel

oranges grocery carts
and sideways apple trees
unicorns are real and all

the dishes are dirty she'll get
around to cleaning them but first
she needs to iron these

leaves into some wax paper
bat-wings in the darkness winging
by the bus stop vampires

with their black-and-white
spectator pumps that's how she
knows armageddon is on its way

the toadstools in the emergency room
where she shouts *I will not lie down!*
I will not! her mother

winces, says *you're hurting my ears*
they're drawing blood from her arm
it comes out thick and dark

why are they doing this to her
the oak door takes phone calls and tells her
be afraid they're giving her something

Rapunzel Missing the Tower

Eternally on the Saw Mill Parkway,
just after sunset, Rapunzel
drives a friend from college home to Brooklyn.

She's forgotten what home is.
Not those cluttered rooms in the tower anymore.
Not those white plaster walls in dormitories

as old as the hoop skirt. That first summer,
house-sitting for a philosophy professor,
she slept in the study. She washed the dishes before she ate.

On campus she took LSD with her boyfriend
and stayed up all night, watching the shadow
of the sprinkler on the ceiling writhe back and forth.

She tries turning off the highway
but the road leads away.
Even in dreams she can't find her way home.

Sometimes she reaches the tower,
but there are no walls, just a spiral
up the side like the Guggenheim,

it's luxury apartments, a retirement home,
a petting zoo. Or she is a baby sitting upright,
chubby arms protruding from a circle of frills.

A cat curls beside her.
She's in a dark cave of redwood
and carpet, a plexiglass bubble in the roof

that lets in one beam of California sun.
Does she remember this or does the photo
she saw in an album now yellowed with age

plant the memory in her mind,
where she finds it unfurling,
telling the story about the place she came from?

What the Crows Do

The crows in the golf course behind campus
know the hospital, know the blood
the nurses took, know the mud, my mind. I blow into the wind
and the wind blows back.

In the hemlock, the crows witness me transfixed
by an icicle, dangling from the tip of a broken branch,
milky-white against bark the color of old blood.
My feet on the pavement, its feet on the tree.

In the courtyard they coax our cat
twenty feet up the trunk of a red oak.
Come down! I yell, and he picks his way
face-first down the bark.

Today the crows huddle in the lee
of the white pines. I'm walking in a thin
curtain of sleet, breathing hard, my spirit rises,
The crows' beaks open

What the Stoner Princess Doesn't Say at Her Job Interview

That for fun she smokes a joint and blasts hip hop
out the window, slouches in her wife-beater.

That she chased her meds one time with an Amaretto sour,
how the barroom twisted.

That she breaks glass when she's mad –
the crash and tinkle.

That her cotton-mouthed rage swells like a toad
every morning.

That she hates the drunk white men
who get kicked upstairs.

That she feels like a fish caught in a weir.
A blueberry caught in a mouth.

A Copy of Szymborska's Collected Poems
Abandoned on a Table

no clocks in the methadone / prison /
rehab
just shuffling
mealtimes with plastic forks no knives
smoke breaks group time et
cetera
we line up and shuffle

szymborska stands
on the balcony in a pencil skirt
looking out over the row houses
maybe all this / is happening in some lab?
she asks

nurses joke about the methadone
they dole it out they call it cocktails
in the med room they stumble
cackle aping its effects

I growl my face hard
this shit
makes you a zombie and then it
kills you
  they get
real serious
apologize

no clocks
just shuffling
the tables
       always sticky

time for crafts!
says the nurse
keys jangling
we line up and shuffle

the real world doesn't take flight
the way dreams do says szymborska
she points me out

I am full and loud with dignity

At the All-Night Diner in New Paltz

The birds have started singing in the dark,
and we've ordered waffles and fried eggs and home fries
after hours of driving aimlessly through the night.
It is Jason Kleinman's birthday,
the summer after my freshman year of college,
and even though I hardly know these people,
we feel fulsome and whole, the five of us.

I have never been this happy sans alcohol or pot,
and the slow motion of the hills as we cross the Hudson
heading back to Poughkeepsie rolls out a corridor of joy,
of adolescent laughter that won't open again
until four years later,

after I end up smoking pot every day
and taking the train two hours to New York City
for interview after interview,
and my girlfriend leaves me for a man she met in a mental institution,
and I quit my crappy job as a transcriptionist for an insurance adjuster,
and my cockatiel flies away while I am packing up the U-Haul,
dragging my sorry ass back to live with my Mom

in shitty Hartford, where I wake up from one more drunk dream
and start going to meetings again, and I find myself
in an all-night diner with some gay men in their 40s,
and we are eating eggs at 10pm
instead of drinking in some smoky club,
and I am laughing again when I least expect it.

A True Account of Talking to the Moon at 3:30 AM in February

after Frank O'Hara

The moon came in my window last night, said,
Hey, why's the heat turned up so high?

Sorry, Moon, I fell asleep after eating all those cookies.

You're not a bear
and winter is almost over anyway.
Get up!

But I'm supposed to be sleeping now.

Who told you that? Some doctor in a lab coat?
You don't have to medicate every sigh and squeal.
You've learned a thing or two
since those early, dark days.

I guess...

Don't guess. Know in the bones of you.
Know with such a certainty that it bursts out of you.
Let the fresh air in when winter loosens its grip.

I'll be hanging pink and fat on the horizon
over a shining river of cars.

Maple Seed Princess

inside each seed an infant waits
    this one grew in spite of me
        turning and turning in the kernel
            of a maple seed
       delicate veins of its sail
in the blood-warm air

I've packed her lunch and her bus pass
    and twenty dollars for emergencies
      she's off to fight city hall and litterers
          she's fiercer than I am
      remembering what happened
   to the young girl I was
the thing that was done to me
       and the lie that followed –

THREE

Lovers Rapunzel Finds in the Wilderness

after Marie Howe

One with skinny hips and rock-hard calves,
licks her till the middle of her bed is soup.
One she finds stomp-dancing in the club,
hooded eyes and lies.
One glitters on the stage,
whispers filthy worship in the back room.
One with a butt so large it's a shelf,
her lovely breasts against her narrow waist.
One dark, and secret, and jealous as an ocean shell.
One large as the devil and twice as wicked.
One a sailboat captain, adjusts the compass
when she would have steered them into the shoals.
One with breasts fine as linen,
milk-blue veins beneath her skin.
One with a smashing wig, wooly curls underneath,
holds her hand and kisses her in public.
One whose boyfriend crashes in the bedroom door,
Rapunzel in nothing but a sheet.
One from Goa, who places
a hotel pillow beneath her to catch the flood.
One whose name she's forgotten.
One whose face she's forgotten. And another.
And another. And another.

little princess becomes a girl

body rising about her like bread   not sure she likes the float
the way the fat wraps   or the grabs from boys

slick and queering slide   the way it pushes her on to class

the moment the throb comes   home sick in her bathrobe
I Dream of Genie on the black&white   blooming red

through the maxi-pads   her mother shows her how to make

the paper towels and scotch tape   rubbing secrets
in the code of her tender   inner thighs

Snow White Awake

The Queen died of course.

Here's her inheritance:
colorful squares of paper, tiny doll heads,
the beaded necklace, the trunks, the heavy furniture.
The castle's forfeit.

Free of the glass box, it's a complicated mess.
Once she woke, the dwarves
took off with the disability check. Prince Charming
stopped texting her.

He used to sing to her,
Rise up, my love, my fair one.

The social worker's useless.
Wandering in the grimy hallway,
looking for a working bathroom,
Snow White considers leaving. Knocks over

a sign on a rolling cart.
Piso mojado. Wet floor.
All that mopping, all that dusting.
The tiny cottage.

I Won't Be Coy Now

for April

Drunken fumbling in the dark – each time I found the wet
center of a woman I withdrew.
I tongued the top of an apple
where the stem met the dimple
and longed to taste.

First time in the light with you,
revelation of your breasts against my face,
your hands on mine, dark on light,
fast curve of your belly,
crease where it meets your hips,

the way you opened and kept opening –
both of us pink on the inside.
You're a natural, you said, and I fell for miles.

Pastoral, Poughkeepsie

I.

I find April tenderly rocking
the breaded thighs in their pan,
and there's collard greens,
and biscuits, and somehow no doubt
she will feed me.
I watch the flesh deepen
to golden brown,
and when I think they're done,
she knows they're not,
and the hunger deepens.

II.

Vassar envelops me in trees,
graceful Gothic arches.
Summers on Sunset Lake,
I watch the trees across the water sway.
I like it in the summers,
all the other students gone away.

April's hair sprouts new dreads
like Tracy Chapman's.
She's round everywhere – cheeks, shoulders,
hips, and breasts. The first time I taste her
is on my futon, seven blocks from campus.
Summer languid in the air.

III.

After Vassar's done with us,
we set up housekeeping on North Clinton Street.
She covers a beat
for the Hudson Valley Black Press.
I cover the rent
in a cheap black blazer, answer phones,
print bill-of-ladings,
send my resume to New York City.
Evenings, I blast hip-hop, hunch
on the front stoop, smoke my joint.

We thought all y'all were dirty, April says,
all you white hippies,
want to get back to the land.
She nestles between my knees
as I twist the roots of her dreads.
We just got off the land.
Summers, my mother picked cotton.
We want clean linoleum, TV.

IV.

Nature's for the very rich,
or at least what I think is rich in 1996.
My '78 Ford Maverick
used to take us to the Vanderbilt Estate,
where sunlight rolled
down a stretch of lawn to the Hudson.
The car junked, we trudge
the streets of Poughkeepsie.

V.

Behind our house, a steep hill
with a Greek temple crumbling at the crest.
I forage raspberry and wild onions. April begins to gasp.
I'm allergic to grass, she says.
I guide her back to bed, hands ranging,
climb hills, pick raspberries,
wild onions of a different kind.

What do you want? she asks one day,
the question deeper than the curl
of pot smoke in our lungs.
I don't stop to think.
A house with a garden.

And you? I ask.
I wanna be married, she says,
but I wanna do what I want.

Dyke March

I.

The red-haired woman is the sexiest,
the dumpling-curved woman,
the Black woman with the high, round ass,
the pale girl with the tattoos
dancing to the punk rock band is the sexiest,
the woman in the shirt the same color
as her peach-pink breasts,
the woman with the thick-framed glasses
holding a sign that says *Follow me
to the Tofu Potluck* is the sexiest.

II.

How many times have I come here,
imposter in my jack-boots or sandals,
bustier or leather jacket? In this immodest
and unlikely air, on the first Friday night
in June, is being a dyke about revolution
or desire? Lying in the grass, I turn to kiss
a woman, her skin like a lyre, her lips
trembling birds, and the revolution disappears,
and just three drops of rain
fall from the summer sky.

With Robin

With other women it was their taste
as I rode them over the crest of the first wave
and then the next

It was a famine of butterflies, a murder of sunflowers, it was
a banner of orange silk that fluttered
at the edge of a cliff and I stepped off and flew

With Robin it was a warm place,
the bottom of the ocean, my body an anemone,
oh, don't move, she said and we hung there

Fat Snow White

Moon curve of her face
around the slant of her black
eyes, lashes whisking over her white
skin stark against her hair,
held back with a crimson bow, swooped
and gathered in two hung-low buns
nestled against her shoulders.

Thin straps of her blue camisole
with their bows, breasts cradled
in cotton, rolls of luscious flesh
rumpling down to the wide bare belly,
navel the dainty landmark of that field,
the curve of her belly that can't help but escape
the simple pleasure of her panties, wide band
of pale flesh folded over the pudenda –
red center, her wrist on the counter
bearing the weight of that body,
braced against the edge of the vanity,
a can of hairspray at the edge of the mirror,
the round shell of the sink, how her heavy thigh
casts a shadow on the concave bowl.

Her elbow shelters against her hip, the red
edge of her panty, delicate inner edge of her forearm
rolls to the iPhone she holds, its bitten apple
just below the camera eye that proclaims
Here is the fairest.

Fox News Princess

Dishes it out but can't take
the extra calories.
Knows a thing or two about two
minutes in heaven with the executive producer.
Always has to show her legs on camera –
heels high, blonde hair blown out,
blood coming from her eyes from her whatever.
Mostly calls her children from the road.
Once had a boyfriend named Mitch.
Truly believes in the cause.
She reports, you decide.
Believes in a return to family value-
menu Fridays at McDonalds, thinks food
stamps are for freeloaders.
Doesn't understand all the fuss about quinoa.
Hates echinacea, takes Tylenol Cold & Flu.
Maybe she's born with it. Maybe it's May-
Day for the communists.
Should the government be in the business
of redistributing wealth? Wonders how much
her male coworkers get paid.
Perches on the Fox & Friends couch,
arms crossed to hide her belly.
Sticks to the talking points, a stickler for details.
Is sick of celery and carrot sticks for lunch.
Attacks the children in a national debate.
Gets fired.
Likes a dirty martini.

FOUR

Rapunzel Trapped in a Tower of Her Own Making

No magicked runes, no post no bills
no letters or fetters, decades later,
she craves a loaf of bread,
but can't put on her shoes.

Sun blesses her through the bay window.
Black-eyed Susans nod outside.
How she longs to stride through the heat,
but the asphalt burns her feet.

She circles in a gyre – the same four rooms,
the lime-green wall she painted to match
the rug the cats have shredded,
rough against bare soles.

Gone the gladiator sandals, the Doc Martens,
the platform boots, only blemished
walking sneakers left, their complicated laces
unravel in her hands.

little princess meets the giant eye

what kind of monster lives outside her safe house
hung high in the tree   a woven basket

a tudor mansion   a bijou cottage   a fancy minaret
she pirouettes   and he just looks at her

assuming it's a he   no mouth to tooth
with toothy teeth   just a giant eye

before the eye   sun breaking through clouds
like on the holy cards   the man on the throne

with the white nightgown   the beard   the priests
in their gilded robes muttering   god caught

in the slant   through the floor-to-ceiling windows
sunlight hovering there   none of that compares

to the giant eye   outside her doorway
a safer monster   maybe

The Marigolds, the River, the Oaks

so much I wanted to love them but
here are some reasons love would not let me
— Adrienne Rich

I once knew all the aspects of bounty, cupping
marigolds in my hands, her petal-skin on my cheek,
her earth-sharp scent, placing the nexus

of the bloom on my tongue, so much
I wanted to love her but there were
so many reasons love would not let me.

He taught me the woods, how to gather acorns,
and dry them, and grind them,
and wash them, and wash them,
to leech the bitter tannins from their flesh.

When I cross the river with him, a sister
gives me seeds of marigolds.
I plant them by the door to bless this new marriage.
But marigolds need full sun.

They grow leggy and strange in the shade of the oaks,
barely blooming though still marigold,
flowers tiny, heart-shaped,
reaching toward a light they barely understand.

A Bit of Earth

On the way to couples therapy, we pass
at least three different barbershops –
one for the Brazilians, and one for the Blacks,
one for the Greeks. Mark goes to a Palestinian
because that's where he was living when we met.

We couldn't afford that neighborhood
so we moved to Roslindale, where we've joined
the tide of white professionals pricing out the families
who have been here since the 40s – Black
and Irish and Italian and Dominican
and French Canadian, and my next-door neighbor
who is a mix of Filipino and Dutch,
and me who is just mixed up.

My partner is the kind of man who *wants*
to go to couples therapy, and cooks dinner,
and empties the dishwasher, so I try to forgive him
for growing up in deluxe Duxbury
instead of St. John's Towers in Stamford.

I used to think growing up a white girl in the projects
meant I couldn't be a racist. Like trading Now&Laters
with Darla Daniels in the lobby of Tower B meant
it would be okay when I asked a Black girl in the high school
bathroom if I could touch her hair. Like it would be okay to
say to my Black professor, *We fixed all that racism
stuff in the 60s didn't we?* Like Mrs. Drugge
with her house in Greenwich with a grand piano
would have driven me to Yale to research a history report
on the tenth-century poet Omar al Khayyam because I was
the sort of girl with potential.

In Roslindale our house has a lawn
and an apple tree
and enough light in the yard to grow vegetables
and every time I plant something in the ground
and know I will be here next year to see it growing
because there is no landlord to raise the rent,
I feel a delicious thrill somewhere between my heart
and the back of my skull.

In our sixth-floor apartment in the Towers,
I tended a hanging garden of spider plants
and Wandering Jew.
High above the asphalt, I learned to pop
the grimy screen, couldn't stand the scrim
between me and the world, however sooty.
Each morning I would greet the great chestnut tree
who spread her limbs across the parking lot,
a world unto herself.
The gingkoes huddled
in their dirt-squares on the sidewalk.
The spare grass huddled on the traffic islands.
The spider plants languished on the windowsill.
The Boston fern died in the dry, winter air.
I read *The Secret Garden*
and imagined my own bit of earth,
and now that I have one I can barely stand
that thrill rising.

I get to see my bulbs come up in the spring
because the government gave my partner
a cheap mortgage for carrying an M-16
around Bosnia, searching for war criminals.
They also sent him to Gitmo after 9-11,
but that's another poem. In the Army,

he had more Black bosses than I've ever had.
I wonder if any of the kids from the Towers
found a way to buy a bit of earth and did they
have to carry a gun to do it.

Nocturne, Roslindale

Night caught in a naked tree – I'm fraught.
The branch will not break.

The two-trunked tree has one root. Rotted apples dropped.
Now, ground frozen, dim memory of flowers.

The bees asleep in their boxed hive,
the honey all slowed in winter's slumber.

Evenings our bodies make two troughs in the bed –
I'm unmade by you.

You swing your leg across mine, two round bodies roll
stop-dropping at the base of a tree, two trunks, January caught

in the branches, light-shade night piling against the glass,
sparrows fluffing in the hedge, their house of branches.

On the Ferry to Spectacle Island

The breeze pushes humid air into something finer
and a young girl in a purple shirt that reads
girl power (n) – the idea of a young girl
being strong and powerful
bends and unbends against the railing.

The girl's voice rises from the stir of conversation, then a man's.
Sharp-dark smell of the boat's diesel engine,
all the buildings of the North End slant past:
brick walls and leaded glass, mansard roofs and slanted roofs.
We slide past a building raised stone by stone in 1708 –
granite blocks and iron balconies,
                              where Elizabeth Bishop might have lived
with her lover, a slight girl in a button-down Oxford
and black capris. Decades ago, in the last century.

In the distance, the Tobin Bridge swoops twice at its highest points,
greened copper, then the boat turns,
presents the cluster of gleaming buildings at the waterfront,
the clock tower of the Customs House,
crown of downtown with its ghosts
of old rebellions, slaves and merchant ships,
the golden lion and the unicorn on the old State House
with a subway in its basement.

Past Fort Point Channel, the glass wall,
of the Federal Courthouse slants above us –
the ferry tour guide says it's meant to be
like a tidal wave of justice over the harbor.
Derricks rise over steel skeletons – the city's
always building on itself. I search for what's left
of the piers

                    where the No Name restaurant
still serves corn and cod, the ghost of the Channel
nightclub where water lapped beneath cracks in the floorboards
and a solid wall of sound
rose gritty and loud above the mosh-pit –
                                        decades ago,
in the last century. Now all gone to condos, bamboo floors,
in-unit washer-dryers, anomie, dyspepsia.

Bright crowds line the quay beneath the ICA.
The boat cuts over sparkles, makes a shush that overlays
the babble of voices all around us,
thrum of the engine, while the sun burns my toes
where I've braced them on the railing,
and a container ship with Yang Ming
inscribed in yellow on its side sports
Lego-block containers full of stereos
and teddy bears from China,
and Castle Island slides past, its earthworks and turf roofs.
Tiny people promenade between the water
and the sunburned grass, and in the distance
the Great Blue Hills lump along
                            with the ghosts
of the Massachusett who named them, the ghosts
of the English who stole them.

The boat roils and rumbles, slowing as it reaches
an island made of two round hills
joined by a spit of land to look like spectacles,
an island that housed a glue factory
                            and then a garbage dump,
and now has green drumlins studded with cottonwood trees
that rustle in the hot July breeze, and there's
a jazz trio on Sundays at the pier, and a snack bar

serving beer and sandwiches, and a bath-house,
and a tiny pebbled beach, and my own round body
bobbing in the waves, with the Boston skyline
orienting me home, over the harbor.

little princess meets the willow

at the mouth of the river   ducks waddle at the water's greasy edge
little princess doesn't want   to stand alone in the lee

of a tree trunk   but the willow
roots where it's planted   reaches its branches up

and out and over   rustles a room with its hang-down leaves
this wild and pliant space   transports her to another willow

rising three stories   above the half-timbered monastery
monks chant in the chapel   the carved and golden

icons shine   incense makes the sunlight solid

little princess   opens up her mouth
and sings

The Window

It knew her breath – that window
in the old white Ford
that carried them from California,
that jumbled and frantic escape.

One long exhale, a frost-white sheen –
her fingertip traced letters on the glass.

Water dripped from those lines,
the words she wrote,
the empty hours in the back
of that battered sedan.

In Utah, a grain from the Great Salt Lake
sailed through the hole in the floorboard
into her mouth, tasting of the sea.

In flat Nebraska, days away from glass towers,
her mother pulled off the highway,
stopped in an empty parking lot,
stretched once, and fell asleep.

Her brother's head in her lap,
no place for her to lie down,
she sat vigil all night,
breathed the window, coded her secrets.

Notes

"Snow White Goes to the Void Seven Times" alludes to Inanna's descent to the underworld. For an English translation of the original Sumerian text, see *Inanna: Queen of Heaven and Earth*, by Diane Wolkstein and Samuel Noah Kramer (Harper & Row, 1983). Some images in the poem were inspired by the TV show *Stranger Things* (Netflix, 2016).

"Lovers Rapunzel Finds in the Wilderness" was inspired by Marie Howe's poem "On Men, Their Bodies," in *Magdalene* (Norton, 2017).

"A Copy of Szymborska's Collected Poems Abandoned on a Table" includes quotations from Wislawa Szymborska's poems "Maybe All This" and "The Real World." Both in *Map: Collected and Last Poems* (Mariner Books, 2016).

"A True Account of Talking to the Moon at 3:30 AM in February" was inspired by Frank O'Hara's poem "A True Account of Talking to the Sun on Fire Island." Anthologized in *Sleeping on the Wing: An Anthology of Modern Poetry with Essays on Reading and Writing.* (Vintage Books, 1982.)

"Fat Snow White" is an ekphrastic of the painting *Mirror Mirror on the Wall* by José Rodolfo Loaiza Ontiveros. An image of the painting appears here: https://laluzdejesus.com/jose-rodolfo-loaiza-ontiveros-profanity-pop-the-laluzapalooza-jury-winners/ (Accessed April 1, 2019).

The epigraph of "The Marigolds, the River, the Oaks" is from Adrienne Rich's poem "Six: Edgelit," in *Dark Fields of the Republic: Poems 1991-1995* (Norton, 1995).

"Nocturne, Roslindale" contains an allusion to James Wright's poem "Two Hangovers," in *The Branch Will Not Break* (Wesleyan University Press, 1963).

Thank you

The love and support of countless poets, friends, and family members have sustained me. First and foremost, thanks to Eileen Cleary of Lily Poetry Review Books for taking a chance on me, and to Christine Jones for helping me make this book the best version of itself.

Special thanks to the students, faculty, and staff of the Lesley University MFA in Creative Writing Program, especially my mentors Sharon Bryan, Kevin Prufer, Adrian Matejka, and Erin Belieu.

Deep gratitude to the donors of the GoFundMe who made it possible for me to attend the Lambda Literary Awards, especially Eryq Ouithaqueue, Beth Charis-Molling, Matthew Wilson, and Rebecca Tapley.

The South Bank poetry workshop has deepened and fed my poetry practice since 2017: Sonja Johanson, Erica Charis-Molling, Sarah Dickinson Snyder, Jenn Martelli, Anna V.Q. Ross, and Christine Tierney. The Po-Biz and Prompts group keeps me trudging past rejections and into free-writes. I am indebted to Carla Drysdale and her book *Little Venus,* where I first saw how it was possible to use alter egos to relate difficult experiences. Many thanks to the many poets who have so graciously allowed me to interview them about their work, including but not limited to Lesley Wheeler, Kwoya Maples, Diane Seuss, Annie Finch, Tom Daley, Carol Hobbs, Enzo Silon Surin, Alexis Ivy, Robert Carr, and Michelle Rogers.

To my mother for always encouraging me to be an artist. To my West Coast family. And to my husband Mark, for all the little things, and the big things too.

About the Author

Frances Donovan's chapbook *Mad Quick Hand of the Seashore* was a finalist for a Lambda Literary Award. Donovan's poems have appeared in *Lily Poetry Review, Solstice, Heavy Feather Review, SWWIM,* and elsewhere. Her interviews of other poets can be found at *The Rumpus* and on her website, www.gardenofwords.com. Donovan holds an MFA in poetry from Lesley University and is a certified Poet Educator with Mass Poetry. In 2019, Boston Poet Laureate Porsha Olayiwola selected one of her poems to be displayed at Boston City Hall. Donovan's work deals with themes of home, family, intergenerational trauma, and sexual and gender identity. She remembers fondly the summer of 1998, when she drove a bulldozer in a Pride parade while wearing a bustier.

www.ingramcontent.com/pod-product-compliance
Lightning Source LLC
Chambersburg PA
CBHW022105020426
42335CB00012B/841